I0199423

Copyright © 2020 by Melanin Grace Publishing, LLC

All rights reserved. No part of this publication may be reproduced, distributed or transmitted in any form or by any means, including photocopying, recording, or other electronic or mechanical methods, without the prior written permission of the publisher, except in the case of brief quotations embodied in critical reviews and certain other noncommercial uses permitted by copyright law. For permission requests, write to the publisher, addressed "Attention: Permissions Coordinator," at the address below.

Melanin Grace Publishing, LLC
P.O. Box 714
Pickerington, OH 43147

ISBN: 978-1-7336439-7-9

For more information and stay connected, please visit **www.janelljonesempowers.com**

Disclaimer
The information provided in this book is not a substitute for professional advice or therapy. The author makes no legal claims, and the material is not intended to replace the services of a certified professional.

The Purpose Healing Life

90-Day Gratitude Journal

Belongs to

____

I IMPACT THE WORLD

Let's dive into gratitude! I want to welcome you and thank you for your time investment.

I am Dr. Janell Jones, I am a bestselling author, international speaker, podcaster, certified life coach, and a licensed clinical therapist.

Don't take giving thanks lightly. I have literally witnessed situations change in my life because I decided to be thankful instead of complaining. When you are thankful, you open the door of abundance.

Being grateful doesn't mean that everything in your life is perfect. Your life is perfect.It means being appreciative for what you do have (no matter how big or small) and offering it up for thanksgiving. This allows abundance to flow in your life and it changes your attitude.

Think about it. Have you ever engaged with an ungrateful person? Did you feel like giving that person anything? I'm sure the negative, unappreciative behavior turned you off.

For the next 90-days, I want to challenge you to shift away from complaining and find things for which to be grateful.

Instructions

It's simple--for the next 90 days, find something for which to be grateful.

1. Use the gratitude journal at night and place it next to your night stand.

2. Challenge yourself to refrain from complaining.

3. Before bed, mentally go through your day and note anything for which you are grateful.

4. Be consistent. You are going to have moments where you don't feel like writing. Do it anyway!

'For I know the plans and thoughts that I have for you,' says the Lord, 'plans for peace and well-being and not for disaster, to give you a future and a hope.'

Jeremiah 29:11

Day 1

Date: ____

Day 2

Date: _____

Day 3

Date: _____

Day 4

Date: ____

Day 5

Date: ______

Day 6

Date: ______

Day 7

Date: ______

Day 8

Date: ______

Day 9

Date: ____

Day 10

Date: ______

Your Super Powers

Write down what you have discovered about yourself

Write down your skills set

Day 11

Date: ______

Day 12

Date: _____

Day 13

Date: ______

Day 14

Date: ______

Day 15

Date: ____

Day 16

Date: ______

Day 17

Date: _____

Day 18

Date: ______

Day 19

Date: ____

Day 20

Date: ______

Day 21

Date: ______

Day 22

Date: ______

Day 23

Date: ____

Day 24

Date: ____

Day 25

Date: ____

Day 26

Date: ____

Day 27

Date: ______

Day 28

Date: ______

Day 29

Date: ______

Day 30

Date: ____

Healing is a choice

DECIDE TO HEAL

Day 31

Date: ______

Day 32

Date: ______

Day 33

Date: ______

Day 34

Date: ______

Day 35

Date: ____

Day 36

Date: _____

Day 37

Date: ______

Day 38

Date: ____

Day 39

Date: ______

Day 40

Date: ______

Day 47

Date: ______

Day 42

Date: ____

Day 43

Date: ____

Day 44

Date: ______

Day 45

Date: ______

Forgiveness

LET IT GO

Day 46

Date: ____

Day 47

Date: ______

Day 48

Date: ______

Day 49

Date: ____

Day 50

Date: _____

Day 51

Date: ______

Day 52

Date: ______

Day 53

Date: ____

Day 54

Date: ____

Day 55

Date: ______

Day 56

Date: ______

Day 57

Date: _____

Day 58

Date: ______

Day 59

Date: ______

Day 60

Date: ____

THINKING OF
The Master Plan

Day 61

Date: ______

Day 62

Date: ____

Day 63

Date: _____

Day 64

Date: _____

Day 65

Date: ______

Day 66

Date: ____

Day 67

Date: _____

Day 68

Day 69

Date: ______

Day 70

Date: ____

Day 71

Date: ______

Day 72

Date: ____

Day 73

Date: ______

Day 74

Date: _____

Day 75

Date: _____

Day 76

Date: _____

Day 77

Date: ______

Day 78

Date: ______

Day 79

Date: _____

Day 80

Date: ______

I am Worthy

I am Wealthy

I am Healthy

I am Creative

Day 81

Date: ____

Day 82

Date: ______

Day 83

Date: ______

Day 84

Date: ____

Day 85

Date: _____

Day 86

Date: ______

Day 87

Date: ____

Day 88

Date: ____

Day 89

Date: ____

Day 90

Date: ______

My Purpose Action Plan

My purpose is:

I help (Who do you help? Be specific-age, gender, demographics, interests, etc):

With (problem you solved):

I do this by (i.e. books, courses, coaching, consultant):

My Purpose Action Plan

The social media platform(s) I used to convey my message is/are:

____

____

____

____

I go live on this platform (Times per week on this/these days):

____

____

____

I network with others (how many times a week)

____

____

I use (what platform) to connect with others:

____

____

____

www.ingramcontent.com/pod-product-compliance
Lightning Source LLC
Chambersburg PA
CBHW050634150426
42811CB00052B/802
* 9 7 8 1 7 3 3 6 4 3 9 7 9 *